Benjamin A. Dobson, Techn. Assoc. Bolton Cotton Mill Mgrs.

Carding Engines and Carding

two papers

Benjamin A. Dobson, Techn. Assoc. Bolton Cotton Mill Mgrs.

Carding Engines and Carding
two papers

ISBN/EAN: 9783337264420

Printed in Europe, USA, Canada, Australia, Japan

Cover: Foto ©Andreas Hilbeck / pixelio.de

More available books at **www.hansebooks.com**

Carding Engines and Carding.

TWO PAPERS

READ BY

MR. ALDERMAN DOBSON, J.P.,

C.E., M.I.M.E., Chevalier de la Legion d' Honneur,

BEFORE THE

MEMBERS OF THE BOLTON COTTON MILL MANAGERS'
TECHNICAL ASSOCIATION.

BOLTON :

G. S. HEATON, PRINTER, VICTORIA WORKS, BOWKER'S ROW.

1887.

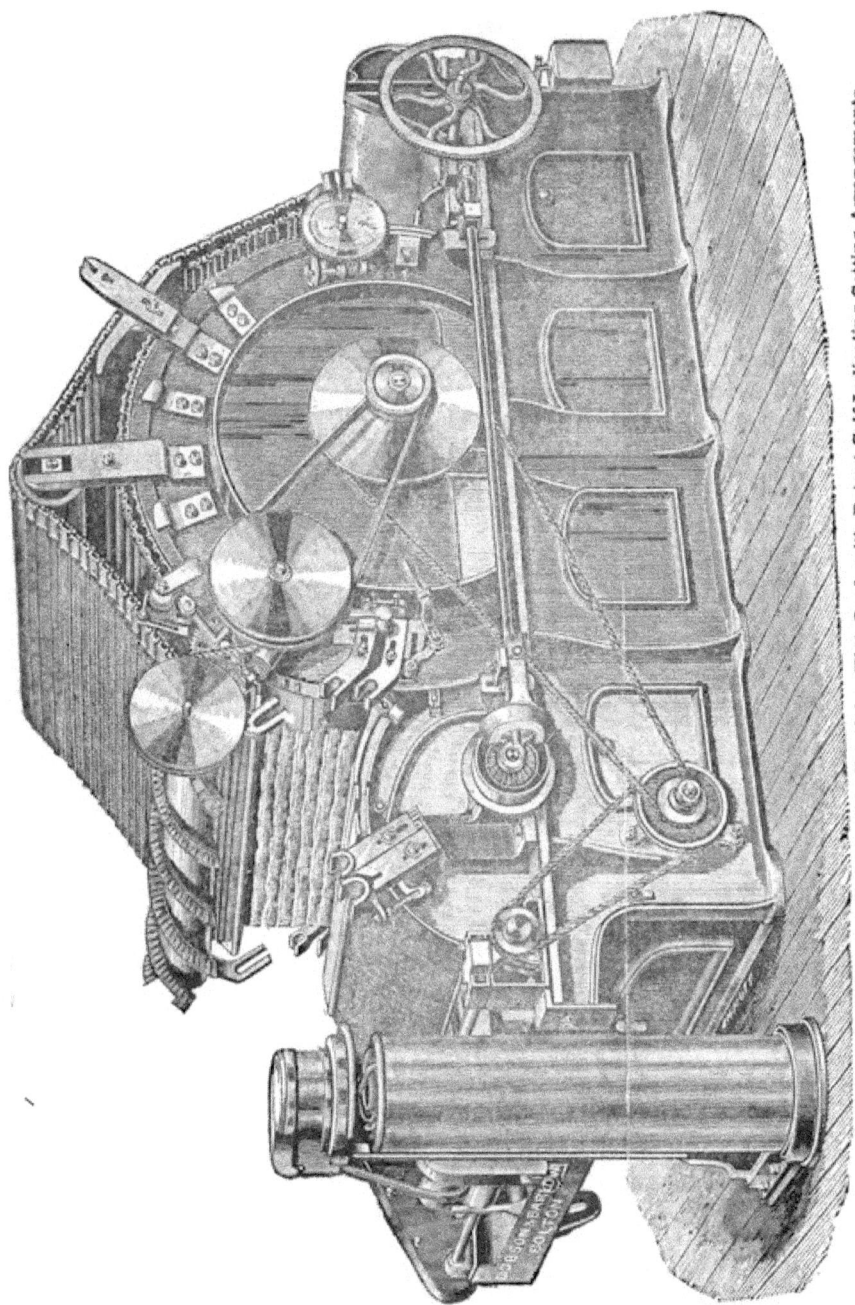

DOBSON & BARLOW'S Patent "SIMPLEX" Revolving Flat Card, with Patent Self-Indicating Setting Arrangements.

SMTI LIBRARY

DOBSON & BARLOW'S Patent "SIMPLEX" Revolving Flat Card, with Patent Self-Indicating Setting Arrangements.

DOBSON & BARLOW'S Patent Improved Mixed Card, with Fixed Plats, Self-Stripped, typical of the Cards used on the Continent.

DOBSON & BARLOW'S IMPROVED ROLLER AND CLEARER CARDING ENGINE.

PAPER READ BY MR. ALDERMAN DOBSON

ON

CARDING ENGINES

BEFORE THE

Members of the Cotton Mill Managers' Technical Association,

April 16th, 1886.

THE necessity for economising the labour in Cotton Spinning of late years has been intensified by the state of depression of Trade which has necessitated Cotton Spinners and Managers searching in every direction the means of reducing as far as possible the expenses attendant upon the production of Yarn. One point that has received particular attention in the whole of the Trade is that of Carding Engines, and this may be divided into two heads, viz.: the construction of the Engine itself, and the character and quality of the Card Clothing used on the Engine. The first Inventor, who seems to have attacked the question of simplicity of regulation in the Carding Engine, was the late Mr. EVAN LEIGH, and his Son, Mr. ARTHUR LEIGH, who, as long ago as 1874, had invented a Carding Engine in which the whole of the Flats were set by the Flexible Bends by one handle, being all brought down or lifted from the Cylinder at one time. Some of these Engines, made by the firm of Messrs. DOBSON & BARLOW, are still at work. A defect in these Machines was the almost impossibility of regulating to the great nicety that is absolutely necessary for good Carding, the height of the Flats from the Cylinder in the whole length of the Flexible Bend. The Card was not much pushed, and was practically abandoned. Different Inventions have been patented from time to time for the purpose of simplifying the setting of the Flats, but the most successful Card made up to recently, that secured an almost perfection of accuracy, was the Card invented by Messrs. ASHWORTH BROS., and of which some Seventy Cards were made by the firm of Messrs. DOBSON & BARLOW. Since then other inventions have been patented, all with the same idea of simplifying the setting, and some of them show considerable mechanical ingenuity, but it is to be feared that the complication of parts and the mechanical impossibility of producing this work in perfection at a price to sell the Card in competition in the present state of Trade would prevent them from ever being marketable articles. The firm of Messrs. DOBSON & BARLOW have been for the last eighteen months studying a method of arriving at this simplicity of setting whilst not complicating the working parts of the Carding Engine, and they have also been thoroughly aware of the necessity of not only improving the method of setting but also of improving the construction, the strength, and the making-up covers of the Cards. The Card made by Messrs. ASHWORTH BROS. has this one great objection : that for its success it is entirely dependent upon the employment of Hardened and Tempered Steel Wire, Needle Pointed, and for this reason, that in order to obtain a selvage at each side of the Card and work a Lap the full width of the Wire; flanges rising above the surface of the Cylinder Wire are applied on each end of the Cylinder between which works the Doffer. This is done with the idea of preventing any blowing out from the edge between the flats and the end of the Cylinder Wire and it may be said. that it fairly well answers its purpose in that respect. However for the purpose of grinding this Wire, these two Discs on the Cylinder Ends have to be removed, and by the hole through which the Cylinder Shaft passes being made much larger than the diameter of the Cylinder Shaft these Discs may be lowered so as to clear the portion of the circumference where the grinding roller is applied. In order to perform this operation 32 screws have to be taken out and replaced. The only place at which these screws can be got at is a hole in the framing below, in one of the panels, which is left there for the double purpose

of getting at these screws and also permitting the escape of
cotton fly that may be rolled between the ends of the Cylinders
and the framing. It will be evident to any practical man that
if this operation had to be repeated as often as necessary to
keep ordinary wire in good condition that this in itself would be
sufficient to condemn the machine. It requires a practical
and skilled mechanic to take off the flanges and replace them,
and even then the fact of tightening some of the screws more
than others is liable to "buckle" the plate so as to make it rub
either against the Doffer or the edges of the undercasings and
thus cause imminent risk of fire.

Furthermore than this another objection is that each
time it is necessary to set the Card, one or two operations are
necessary, the Cylinder is mounted in Phosphor Bronze Steps
supported by a screw pillar passing through the framing and
worked by a square at the end below the framing, the end
screw on each side being fastened up by means of a cover and
lock and key. This method of raising the Cylinder to the flats
is perhaps correct practically, although not theoretically, but
for one or two difficulties. In the first place, this also requires
a person of special training to do correctly, as the operation
is one of great delicacy ; and in the second place, the economy
of room in a Cotton Mill at the present day would scarcely
allow Cards to be placed sufficiently far apart to perform the
operation with comfort, safety, and convenience. The other
method of setting the flats is by removing a strip of rolled steel,
which surrounds the circumference of the turned bend upon
which the flats travel, and replacing it with one of lesser
thickness, thus allowing the flats to be placed nearer the
Cylinders. Practically, if these operations could be performed
with absolute accuracy, perhaps no exception could be taken
to them on the score of exactness, but a trivial variation of the
thickness of the steel strips that might be replaced, the amount
of tension placed on these strips to fasten them down to the
circumference of the Bend, which is done by means of drag
screws and nuts attached to front and back of the Bend, is
sufficient in some cases to prevent that accuracy of setting that

is considered so necessary. There is furthermore the difficulty
that in a large number of these Cards some of these points may
be overlooked, and the fact that once the Cylinder being
moveable, in respect to its horizontal axis, if left half a turn too
much up or down by one of these mistakes, which would easily
occur, would practically render it impossible to know whether
the Card Cylinder was or was not perfectly true.

This is a practical difficulty which I think few men
occupying a responsible position in Cotton Mills, in these
difficult times, would care to face. It has been said by the
Makers of these Cards that they profess and determine to keep
them in order themselves, but I think I will have the sense of
most practical men with me when I say that no man who
respects himself would be content to leave the setting of his
Cards to the absolute will and discretion of an outsider. It is
evident then that these Cards for the ordinary purposes of
Cotton Mills would be unsuitable for the reason that their
practicability is absolutely dependent upon the character
of the clothing employed. Inasmuch as an ordinary class of
wire demanding frequent grinding and consequent frequent
setting would make it impossible to work these Cards in any
number. This question of Clothing is one of great importance,
but I do not propose to go into that in detail on this occasion,
inasmuch as it opens up questions of experience so varied that
it would require at least two evenings to do justice to it. I
will however proceed to describe the Carding Engine recently
perfected and completed by Messrs. DOBSON & BARLOW. I
will premise that this Carding Engine contains all the elements
necessary for the production of really good work, inasmuch as
special patterns have been constructed with a view of so
strengthening the whole of the framing and the various parts
that there may be an entire absence of deflection or vibration.

The Carding Engine consists of the ordinary framing,
strengthened with a large diameter of Cylinder Shaft made in
hard Cast Iron. The Cylinder Shaft Journals turn in
Phosphor Bronze Bushes, half an inch thick which are secured

in a pedestal cast in one piece with the Bend. From this pedestal the Bend is turned in a lathe outside, inside and on the top surface. Templets are provided for the purpose of drilling the holes in these Bends, necessary to take the various Brackets that are placed thereon. Each Bolt is counter sunk on the inside to fit perfectly level with the surface, and being turned to templet and chased in a lathe in the screw part, the Bolt not only acts as a Bolt, but also as a steadying pin, and the accuracy with which this work can be executed by these templets is shown by the fact that in no case has there been even a deviation of more than one five hundredth part of an inch, and even this very exceptional variation is due to the variable character of the metal; the Brackets are themselves milled to templet and drilled and bored to templet, and any one Bracket can be taken off and placed on to another bend with the absolute certainty that there will be no variation measurable. The Setting is done in the following manner: The Flexible Bend which has been very considerably strength-ened is supported on five points by steel case hardened pins, and is held between Brackets turned on the inside, and the turned face of the Bend, so that the Flexible Bend is held between two turned surfaces, and there can be no vibration laterally. The portion of the Flexible immediately over the Doffer is held by a short link which is free to swivel on its centre, and the three intermediate setting-points are Brackets, having on them a curve which theoretically and actually represents the travel of a point upon the Flexible Bend, traced by its motion longitudinally and radially. These curves are cut by a Milling Machine with a copying apparatus, the copy being three times the size of the finished work, thereby reducing the elements of error. At the side over the Lickerin is the real setting points. There is a finely cut rack in phosphor Bronze inserted into the end of the Flexible, into which works a Steel or phosphor Bronze wheel, on the end of which is a wheel of 160 teeth, finepitch; a worm working into this carries on the end of its shaft another worm wheel of 30 teeth, and this is connected across the card by a shaft between the upper and lower flats, There is an Index Wheel marked with engraved explanations showing the amount of setting that has taken place. The Dial is marked in fiftieths of an inch, and each fiftieth of an inch will represent somewhere about the two thousandth part of an inch of downward movement of the flats; this means that practically each turn of the setting handle only represents one eight thousandth part of an inch of movement of the flat. The end of this shaft is fastened by a lock and key, and as it is at the end of the Card immediately over the Lickerin, there would in no case be any difficulty in obtaining sufficient access to set. The setting apparatus can of course, be placed on either side of the Card as may be most convenient, and would preferably be placed on that side where the driving pulleys are, on account of there being more room between the Card which is set and its neighbour, or each side can be set independently if required. This apparatus has proved thoroughly reliable, and both practically and theoretically correct ; in no case has a variation of more than a five hundredth part of an inch been found to exist, which can be taken as sufficiently correct for a working apparatus, and it is to be hoped that even this difference of one five hundredth part of an inch will cease to exist by even yet improved experience.

Now I will at once proceed to say that the only importance to be attached to this method of setting is the fact that absolute accuracy can be obtained, that it is simpler and only one setting is required, and that it will be quite practicable for a Manager of a large Mill to set the whole of his Cards in a very short space of time, and having possession of the key himself would know that by no means could meddling workmen alter the setting. At the same time it must be freely conceded when all is said and done there is really no great difference in any of these methods as regards result, of setting flats over the old arrangement of the Revolver Card, where there were three drag screws and two intermediate supports in all five setting points to each flexible. When these Cards were in the hands of thoroughly skilful and reliable men, (and whatever may be said on this point by interested persons) the whole advantage

was one of simplicity and facility, and none of these arrangements will produce one ounce more production or any better
quality of work than the old Card, except in so far as the
advantages I have already enumerated, but above and beyond
this question of setting the Card I am describing made by
Messrs, Dobson & Barlow contains a number of improvements
which are really of practical utility as regards production and
quality.

Some considerable time ago this firm took out a patent
for an improved Cover between the Doffer and Cylinder, and
this improvement was forced upon them by the continual
complaints of Cotton Spinners that Cotton Fly would collect
in the interstices in the cover or covers, and that when of a
sufficient volume, would be caught by the Cylinder or Doffer,
and come out in the "Webb" or "Fleece" in the front, in
the shape of thick cloudy places from time to time. This
defect in their Card has been absolutely cured once for all by
the adoption of this patent Cover. This Cover is of steel in
three parts, one, the portion that descends between the Doffer
and the Cylinder is planed and polished so as to afford no
chance of cotton catching and forming "Cat Tails." It is
hollow in the inside to form a box to allow the strippings from
the flats to fall into it. There is a steel cover hinged to this
box in such a manner that there is no joint visible next to
the Cylinder on the inside, and it has also a cover hinged
to it in the front to cover it to the centre of the Doffer.
This whole cover is carried upon two plates which are turned,
and which are carried in their turn on the noses of the Bend.
These noses are turned also to the radius of the outside of the
Cylinder Bends, and are provided with horizontal slots and
drag screws, so that the whole cover can be set to the greatest
nicety to the wire of the Cylinder and Doffer. The Steel
Cover spoken of just now shuts down upon what is known as
the front flat knife, a piece of steel plate fixed to a plate of
Cast Iron, and planed to a sharp knife edge ; the object of this
plate as is well known being to avoid blowing out and to regulate
the amount of waste made, the joint is closed by an inserted

strip of steel. The back of the Card is treated in the same manner. There is a steel plate planed to two fine knife edges which sets up between the flats and the Cylinder Wire when the flats are going on to the Cylinder, and also close down between the Lickerin Wire and the Cylinder Wire. This plate is fastened to a strong Cast Iron plate, which is furnished on the outside with flanged covers at the outside of the Bend to prevent blowing, and also with set screws, so that this cover can also be regulated with the greatest accuracy to the wire of the Cylinder. The Lickerin Cover is made to fit against the plate just named, and down close over the feed roller. The feed roller is on the " Dish " principle, and has been very considerably strengthened to avoid deflection, which, strange to say, has been found to exist in nearly all Cards manufactured ; this is now absolutely rigid. The clearer employed is of the revolving character, and effectually prevents accumulation of waste on the feed roller, or any blowing out.

The Grinding Fixings are also an improvement which allows Messrs. DOBSON & BARLOW to get as many flats on a straight framing as can be got by other makers on what is termed a " set down " framing. Thus, on this Card as spoken of there are 110 flats on a straight framing, neither Doffer nor Lickerin being set down ; the consequence of this is a very important improvement in the quality of the work, owing to the extra number of flats at work and the fact of the Cylinder, Doffer, and Lickerin being on the same level framing. For instance, in order to grind or strip this Card the following would be done :—The Grinding Fixings slide in planed sides, and are fixed originally to a certain height radially to the centre of the Cylinder Shaft, in such a way that there is no room for variation subsequently. When these slides are on their bottom bed the two bearings for the Grinding Roller are precisely level and parallel horizontally with the Cylinder Shaft. When the Grinding Roller is put in it can be set on either side, in or out, as may be necessary, but such a thing as getting the Grinding Roller cross-wound is absolutely impossible. This is in itself a security for better grinding, and

inasmuch as this grinding takes place almost over the extreme
lateral point of the circumference of the Cylinder, any vibration
or variation will be up or down, and not sideways, and therefore not affect the correctness of the grinding to the same
degree as if the Grinding Roller were higher up. DOBSON &
BARLOW have also other excellent grinding arrangements. With
the Doffer grinding similar dispositions are taken, and the
grinding fixings are planed from the bearing of the Doffer, and
being cast in one piece with it variation is impossible. In grinding the Cylinder it is only necessary to turn down the hinged
portion of the front cover, then the framing allows the Grinding
Roller to traverse over, and after grinding, to brush out, it is
only necessary to lift the slide blocks on either side of the Card
by a handle provided for this purpose, up to the top stop, and
then the supports are in their exact position, and the Stripping
Out Brush can be set in or out. The opening caused by the
turning down in this cover is also sufficient for stripping purposes, and when it is requisite to set the Doffer to the Cylinder,
all that is necessary is to swing the cover back upon its two
supporting plates until the catch on each side drops into a
groove, and then the cover is safely retained whilst setting pro-
ceeds. When the Doffer is thoroughly set, all that is necessary
is to lift the catches on either hand, and allow the plate to slide
quietly down to its bearings; this can be done by one man.
One effect of this particular arrangement of covers has been
that drafts in the inside of the Card have been avoided to such
an extent that it is now possible to Card a lap the full width of
the Cylinder Wire, and in fact rather more, say three-quarters
to one inch wider. The selvage being perfect there is no
necessity for arrangement of flanges, as described in the
beginning of this paper. It will be noticed that there is no
wood employed in the construction of this Card whatever, the
Linings or Sweeps as they are called, surrounding the
Cylinder are part of the Bends, and turned in the lathe at the
same time. There are no covers of wood, and in fact the
whole of the interior of the Card is planed and polished.

What I contend is the advantage of a Card constructed

on the principles such as I have described is, that it is not dependent upon any particular class of wire, and can be set as practically and as advantageously for the ordinary iron wire as for steel, hardened and tempered, and needle-pointed.

This Card will easily produce ten per cent. more work than any ordinary Card, on account of the possibility of working the whole width of the wire, that is to say, $41\frac{1}{2}$ ins. as against 38. On the other hand there is a clear ten per cent. of Carding gained in the extra number of flats, as there are 44 flats always fully at work. There is a further improvement in connection with this Card, viz., that of the Dofling Comb Motion, and I will now proceed to read the advantages of this improved Comb Motion.

A fair speed of Cylinder for a Card of this description, and when working cotton that will stand it, is 160 revolutions per minute.

There is a Card at present at Messrs. Dobson & Barlow's Works which is Carding American Cotton at the rate of 850 lbs. per week of Mill hours, and of course this production is not the extreme limit, but what is considered as a fair practical production for the quality desired.

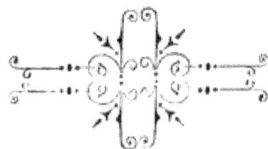

IN continuance of my former paper on Carding and Carding Machines it would be well perhaps to go to the origin of Carding with a view of tracing some of the successful alterations that have beem made with a view to improve this process of the Cotton Manufacture. In the primitive days of Cotton Spinning there was no such thing as a Carding Engine, and the Cotton when imported was extremely costly and was very carefully treated. At the same time, the Cotton in those days was most decidedly of better quality stronger and longer staple, and much cleaner than the cotton of the present day. In those days it was sufficient to parallelize the fibres of the Cotton and to form them into a thick web or sliver. The question of removing dirt or short fibre had not then the importance that it has at the present day. It would almost seem as if Cotton had deteriorated in quality as it has increased in quantity. No doubt competition asserts itself as formidably in Cotton growing as it does in Cotton Spinning, and with a result at least as unfortunate as regards quality. The primitive Carding was done by a series of Cards fastened on a table or bench upon which the Cotton was lightly spread with the fingers and the operative then took a Card mounted on a small board to which was affixed a handle, and by drawing this carefully and lightly over the Cotton, succeeded in stretching the cotton fibres in a somewhat parallel condition. The Cotton in this condition was taken off in the shape of a fleece with what was then termed a needlestick. The first mechanical arrangement contrived for the suppression of this hand work and the obtaining of a continuance of the Card sliver was an immense jump from the original idea of Carding to the idea that now obtains generally with regard to the proper duties which may be expected from a Carding Machine.

Whether it was Lewis Paul or Bourn who really invented the Carding Machine it is difficult now to say, but it would almost seem that the principle of Carding was worked out in two different directions by Bourn and Paul. Bourn seems rather to have arrived at the idea of the Roller Card, whilst Paul seems to have taken the principle of the fixed Flat Card as his model. This Card however was not introduced into Lancashire until 1760, and the first Carding Engine which produced a continuous web stripped with a doffing comb, and contained both rollers, clearers, and flats with a Doffer and Condenser in the front, and fed by a Lap behind, certainly seems to have been that of Sir Richard Arkwright, one of which, with top flats, can now be seen in the Chadwick Museum, Bolton. This is perhaps the most elementary Carding Machine extant, and is certainly well worthy of a careful inspection by any person interested in the Cotton Industry. I have just mentioned this casually with a view of showing that even in the original inception of Carding Engines that there were two ideas with regard to Carding. The original system of Carding by hand Cards may be taken to represent the Roller and Clearer Card ; at the same time there is a certain similarity in the placing of the fibres parallel with those Cards on the Flat system, but in this case there was almost contact of the two wires, and the Cotton was only saved from severe injury by the fact that there was no great surface speed and the hand pressure yielded to any resistance, thereby saving the fibre from being cut and torn, and as the Cards were not ground to the present degree of sharpness there was from that reason less chance of excoriating the fibre. With the hand Carding, grinding was not necessary, inasmuch as the Carding process could be repeated time after time until complete without removing the fleece, and the Cotton being worked between smooth points of wire, the resulting friction of the wires and also the friction of the fibres of the Cotton one upon the other replaced to an extent, the action due to the speed of the Cards of the present day. Later on, adjustable guides were fixed to the sides of the table, and these were regulated to prevent contact of the wires. When this was done it became necessary to grind the wires to give holding power to the points, and this was done by a hard sandstone or hone. The first Card made by Arkwright seems to have combined most of the best principles of Carding that are known at the present day. The Cotton was taken from the Lap through a pair of feed rollers by the main cylinder, which was covered with sheets on the old principle of Clothing Cards. There were then two rollers and two clearers, which almost worked in contact with the Cylinder, nothing but bare clearance being allowed, the Cotton being worked and re-worked, being each time made more parallel than before. The work of parallelizing and further cleaning the Cotton was performed by a small number of fixed flats which were between the Doffer and the last Clearer, the Doffer being stripped with a comb, and the sliver taken away almost in the same form as at the present day. There have been endless varieties of Carding Engines since then. There have been Roller and Clearer Cards of all descriptions' some with Rollers and Clearers, others with Rollers only, acting simply as Revolving Flats, being Rollers turning slowly on their own centres and being stripped each one by a comb. Composition Cards with Rollers and Clearers and Flats, and Cards of Fixed Flats, and lastly the Revolving Flat Card. It would take very much longer time than I have at my disposal to go into the various descriptions of Cards that have been practically worked in Cotton Mills, but I should like to reason with regard to the improvements that have been made, and also the direction in which they have been made. When Cards were used first on the Roller and Clearer principle it would almost seem as if the Card would do its work better if the Cylinder was running at a moderate speed, and the Rollers and Clearers running more quickly, inasmuch as the Carding process consisted in the points of the wire on the Rollers and Clearers taking away the Cotton either from the Cylinder or the Roller at a difference of circumferential speed sufficient to obtain the smoothing or stretching effect upon the fibre, this being repeated by lifting the Cotton fibres somewhat parallel, and in the stretching over the points of these various organs of Carding, some of the short fly is driven into the interstices in the Cards, and some of the moats and leaf have also been lodged there, therefore in the Roller Card it is necessary to strip the Rollers, Clearers, and Cylinders, and Doffer at certain times to avoid too much accumulation of dirt in the wire. The difference between a Card of this description and the fixed flat Card would seem to be that where there are fixed flats it is necessary that the Cylinder should run very much more quickly than in the other case, in order that the centrifugal force given by the speed of the Cylinder should replace the action of the Rollers and Clearers with regard to stretching the fibres and making them parallel. As a matter of fact it is within the knowledge of any man, who is experienced in a Cotton Mill, that the action of the Flat Card is more efficacious and efficient as regards the parallelizing of the fibres than the Roller Card, and for this reason that the speed of the Cylinder being sufficient, the Cotton being held at one end by the Cylinder Wire, as soon as it comes under the influence of the first flat, it is by centrifugal force thrown against the " Toe " of the flat, and on its progress, due to the revolution of the Cylinder is, you may say, combed down by the bevil in the flat, as far as the " Heel." This is repeated from flat to flat, the space between the flats being sufficient to allow the cotton to fly away from the Cylinder by the centrifugal action, so that in no part is the surface of the flat lost but the effect is the same for every flat. If there were no spaces between the flats, or no bevil in the setting of the flats, the Cotton taken from the Lickerin would have no chance of changing its position, and being therefore operated upon in all senses by the flats, and this of course is quite necessary in order to have clean smooth sliver. This will show you the benefit of the inclination or bevil of the flats and also the necessity of having a space between the wire of each flat. If the Cotton is properly opened and properly placed upon the Cylinder by the Lickerin then the action that must, and does take place is the process of the Cotton being drawn over the surface of the flat wire, and that the moats and neps, and short Cotton are held by the flat wire, and consequently the flats require stripping at certain intervals. As you will be aware, this has been accomplished in many various ways.

You will however see that the action of this continued combing from the back flat to the front means, that according to common sense, coarser wire is required at the first flat, and the finest wire at the last flat, so that the wire should change gradually finer every five or six flats, in order that the process may be equivalent to that of the action of the circular comb in the Combing Machines where the tangled, matted Cotton is first attacked by open coarse Combs, and as it is opened by these is gradually followed by finer Combs. This, as a matter of principle, is undeniable. The flats being fixed in position, it is possible to set very close so as to practically *Comb* with the last three or four flats over the Doffer, and smoother Carding can be obtained when this is carefully attended to than on any other description of Machine. The Revolving Flat Carding Engine is of course on the same principle with regard to the action of the Cotton, with this difference, that the bevil of each flat is the same, the number of the wire of each flat is the same, and instead of the flat being stationary the flat is moved in the same direction as the Cylinder. Now to my mind this peculiar action of the movement of the flat when leaving the Cylinder will account for what I believe is now recognised as a fact, that the same lustrous Yarn cannot be made from the Revolver Flat Card as from the ordinary fixed flat even with same make of wire. It is well known to most practical men that in either wood cutting or iron milling or cutting, that it is necessary that the work to be cut should proceed in the direction opposite to that of the cutter, so that sufficient clearance may take place after each tooth has done its work. No difference of speed can effect this principle, and I maintain that although to a less extent, the same thing holds good in Carding, and that were it possible to keep the Revolving Flats stationary, the work would be smoother and better, because in leaving the Cylinder the flat that has worked the Cotton at that particular moment has a tendency to lift the fibres from the surface of the Cylinder, of course allowing it to fall down again, but it is put on the Doffer in a more tangled condition than it would otherwise have been, and instead of the fine combed action that ought to take place with the last flat, the flat being moved in the same direction as the Cylinder prevents this to a very great degree in spite of the great difference of circumferential speed. This is perhaps the most serious defect the Revolving Card possesses. It has been asked, why not run the flats in the other direction? This has been tried with the natural result that the flats travelling off the Cylinder over the Lickerin took off a large percentage of good Cotton which had never been carded and which was sent into waste, besides this, there was the difficulty of stripping the flats which is practically impossible.

The improvement that has most conduced to good single Carding and large productions, has been the employment of the Lickerin covered with Inserted Sawtooth Wire, and the employment of the Dish Feeder. These two elements of Carding are old in themselves, both having been known for the last thirty years, and perhaps more than that, but having been badly made, and improperly understood, did more harm than good for a considerable time. However, some years ago there was a necessity for improvement in Carding, and one of the first things done was to employ the Sawtooth Lickerin, and when this was done it was found that a more exact feed was required than the old system of two feed rollers could give, and " Bodmer's " feed, as it was then called, was employed. There was an idea extant that it was impossible to Card a good class of Cotton with this Dish Feed, and the Lickerin Sawtooth Wire, as it was thought the action was too brutal for fine fibres, and loss of strength to the yarn would ensue. It is undoubted that it would be possible to cut the cotton to powder if an improperly arranged Lickerin and Dish Feed were used, on the other hand, I may here point out, that short of wilful action, no damage can be done to the Cotton, and it is to be presumed, that all makers of machinery are aware of the importance of this point and study it. The effect of the Lickerin covered with this wire as compared with the old Lickerin, covered with sheets working at the feed by two feed rollers, is this, that in the ordinary Lickerin sheet wire, it was impossible to strike down the heavy dirt with the same

certainty and ease that it is now done, and the tendency was
for the Lickerin to get choked, and this required constant
stripping and grinding and made perhaps more neps than any
other portion of the Card. As you are aware now, the
Lickerin never wants grinding, and is always in a condition to
do its work without waste or flocking, and as the principle of
gradual progression is employed in the arrangement of these
parts, the thick portion of the Cotton is never attacked by the
wire of the Lickerin, but the extreme ends of the thick portion
of the lap are just combed out by the extreme points of the
Lickerin wire and as the Cotton is fed forward, the heavy dirt
and fly are knocked out by the front teeth of the Lickerin wire
and the Cotton is gradually combed as it becomes thinner and
thinner, until at length the Cotton is taken away by the
Lickerin wire, without strain or stress and carried forward, and
placed on the Cylinder. The knives employed under the
Lickerin are a particular and great improvement with regard
to determining the amount of fly and dirt that should be taken
out, and if these are properly set, any dirt adhering to the
Cotton fibre after being loosened from the feed part should be
scraped off by the action of these sharp knives. Of course,
this has eased the work of the Carding Engine itself to a very
great extent, as the heavy work is done entirely by the Lickerin
which was not so in olden times, and it therefore may be said
that the improvements in the Lickerin have contributed more
than anything else to the large out-turns of the present day,
and above all, to the possibility of spinning good 60's twist
from single Carding. Seventeen years ago, all the mills in the
Bolton district had double Carding and four fly frames, now
there is not one mill double Carding and few with four frames.
This is of course an immense economy of labour. As a proof
of the difficulty that existed with the old Lickerin, I may
mention that many inventions have been made, particularly
abroad, for the purpose of keeping the Lickerin clear. I have
seen one roller, two rollers, and even three rollers working in
different combinations *under* the Lickerin, the object being to
prevent the Lickerin from placing on the Cylinder Cotton in
lumps pulled from the feed part, as the roller under the

Lickerin, running slowly against the wire of the Lickerin itself, caused a certain Carding part to help to open any lumps or thick Cotton that might be taken in by the Lickerin, and any Cotton thus dealt with was taken by this slow running intermediate to the fast running rollers underneath which ran in contact with the intermediate rollers and the Cylinder. Its action was supposed to be that of stripping the main Cylinder, and it was consequently termed, " Continuous Cylinder Stripper." I may say that I have seen Cards on this principle that have run four days without being stripped out, and which when stopped seemed fairly clean, but I should not on this account like to recommend any of my friends to adopt such a course or system, as we find the inconveniences attending it very much more than overweigh the advantages. One other organ of Carding which was employed when the old Lickerin was in existence still holds its own and is very useful for dirty Cottons, and that is what is known as the Dirt Roller over the Lickerin. This is a roller running very slowly and clothed with diamond pointed angular wire set close to the Cylinder immediately above the Lickerin, and revolving slowly from the Lickerin, perhaps one turn in an hour, sometimes more sometimes less. This roller is automatically stripped by a Comb, and its object is to take moats and leaf and some short Cotton from the main Cylinder. If this roller is properly understood and properly set it is capable of easing the work of the flats to an *enormous* extent, and for dirty Cottons as I have said is almost invaluable. In its original inception it was placed on the card for the purpose of remedying the bad work of the Lickerin, and even now, that the Lickerin is found to do its work so much better, there is a distinct advantage in some cases in employing this roller. There have been also numerous experiments with the view of avoiding the necessity of stripping the Cylinder. One known as " Higgin's " Stripper was perhaps the most successful and consisted in one roller running in contact with the Cylinder, and which roller had an alternate speed, one slower than the Cylinder, the other faster, the strap being shifted from one speed to the other by cams. The object of this was for a certain number of minutes this roller should over-run the Cylinder and strip the material out of it. Then the Cylinder in its turn was supposed to strip this roller, and no doubt both organs to a certain extent did their work, but it simply meant that this dirt was taken in and that a certain portion of it went through with the web, making bad work in the Card Room, and increasing the amount of fly in the mill generally, and that in order to have clean Carding it was necessary after all to stop the Cylinder to strip it. The Carding from an engine furnished with this Stripping Apparatus was always irregular, and it would be well understood that it should be so. Of course the important question with regard to Carding is the nature of the wire that is employed to cover the various organs of Carding, but this enters into a different phase of the question, and one which I should prefer to leave over for another occasion. The shape of the section of the wire, the angle, and the length of the two portions of the tooth, the nature of the foundation, and the point achieved by grinding ought to enter into the question of the quality of Carding. In connection with the matter of the Carding Machine itself, there is the question of the speed that the Card should be run to do its work most efficiently. Some few years ago it was the opinion that 130 to 140 revolutions per minute was a fair speed for a 45 in. Cylinder—at the present day many people are running their 50in. Cylinders at 180, and some persons have gone even further and recommended 190 or 200. I think many gentlemen present will remember the time when Cards with 45in. Cylinders only ran 140, and they will, I think, admit that when this was the case that the Carding was certainly as clean, and the yarn stronger and smoother. There is no advantage without its drawback, and the improvements that have been made in the construction of Carding Engines have undoubtedly caused a certain inconvenience. There is more fly, the yarn is rougher, and it is seriously to be questioned whether the yarn made now-a-days is as strong, out of the same quality of Cotton, as was made 30 or 40 years ago. When a certain speed is reached the centrifugal action of the revolving parts of the Carding Engine cause a very disturbing influence on the draughts of air that are always to be found in machinery in motion, and these draughts are specially prejudicial to the action of carding, but it may be fairly stated, that with a Card properly made and properly enclosed, that 180 revolutions per minute is a practical speed so far as the merely mechanical portion of the operations of Carding is concerned. It will, of course, require years of careful experiment before the relative advantage of the different speeds can be arrived at, but in the meantime I should strongly advise any person interested, not to lend themselves to exaggerations of either speed or production.

I have said nothing in this paper with regard to Undercasings, but their importance is generally recognised and I may say that the form of Undercasing brought out originally in Bolton, and which has been adopted in nearly all the Bolton Mills has also come to be adopted by other makers in England and abroad. This, I think, is a good proof of the correctness of the principle upon which they are made. There is no tendency for fly to collect anywhere, and all the knives are made so accurately that the whole Undercasing can be set to the Cylinder almost as accurately as a flat. The number of the bars, their distance apart, and the amount of blank sheet iron that may be placed in any portion of the Undercasing is of course determined by the nature of the Cotton, and the amount of fly that it is allowable to make in the operation of Carding, but in the latest make of Cards such a thing as an accumulation of fly at any portion of the working part of the Card is, and ought to be entirely unknown. If the transition of Carding machinery is carefully followed, it will be found that there has been very little improvement in principle since the first Carding Engine was made, and what improvements there have been brought out, have been principally improvements in detail of construction, extra solidity and rigidity of the parts, and until some method of dealing with Cotton by electric force, or some kindred force can be discovered, we must confine ourselves to perfecting small details, and obtaining as far as possible perfection of construction. I consider that the question of grinding Cards should properly be treated of in a paper on the Card Wire, but from the Machine Makers' point of view it is very important that the grinding fixings should be on a scientific principle. I myself was, I think, the first individual in England to bring this matter forward and it was in consequence of the importance I saw attached to it in the manufacturing districts abroad, particularly in Alsace, and the result of it has been that the grinding fixings on the Cards made by my own firm are always set radially to the Cylinder and Doffer, so that it is out of the power of any workman to get his grinding roller crosswise. He may set his roller in too much at one side, but it will always be absolutely parallel with the axis of the Cylinders and Doffers.

The question of the advantage, or otherwise of the slow grinding, for which my firm possess a patent, is also one of questionable position at the present moment. It is contended by those who have had considerable experience that the advantage gained by slow grinding is counterbalanced by the fact that owing to the slow speed of the movement of Cylinder and Doffer, the wire is too long in contact with the grinding apparatus and a heat is caused which tends to soften the wire and certainly causes it to be hooked in iron wire, and to take the " temper " out of hardened and tempered steel wire. As I said, however, this question is one that has occurred to be dealt with, and I think would properly come under the head of Card Clothing.

The following calculations taken from an ordinary instance of a Card, Carding Egyptian Cotton in a Bolton Mill, will perhaps be interesting as showing the amount of Cotton fed in and taken out of the Card, and the approximate thickness of the layer of Cotton on each part of the Card :—

Weight of Lap, per yard		10 ounces.
Speed of Feed Rollers, per minute	...	1 revolution.
„ Lickerin, „		400 revolutions.

Waste made under ditto ...		...	2 per cent.
Speed of Cylinder, per minute			160 revolutions.
Waste made on Cylinder ...		...	2 per cent.
„ on Flats ...	...	...	3·5 „
Speed of Doffer, per minute ...			12 revolutions.

The compressed thickness of the Lap may be taken as $\frac{1}{17}$in., and the thickness of the layer of Cotton may be taken as follows:—

On Lickerin $\frac{1}{5141\frac{1}{77}}$in.

„ Cylinder ... $\frac{1}{10950\frac{1}{570}}$in.

„ Doffer $\frac{1}{5307}$in.

This will show that the Cotton on the working parts of the Card cannot be continuous, but consists of fibres and aggregations of fibres, with large spaces and intervals between. The thickness of a fibre of ordinary Egyptian Cotton is $\frac{1}{1570}$in. so that the extent of space of Carding Wire, as compared with the surface covered with Cotton, may be taken as:—

For Lickerin 23·5 to 1.

„ Cylinder 50·8 to 1.

„ Doffer 1·86 to 1.

I supplement the above calculations by a table showing the speeds, working parts, the circumferential speed, and the proportionate speeds, the points of wire under different circumstances with the numbers, and also the number of fibres on the working parts. *(See last page.)* From this it will be seen that the number of points at work on that portion of the Card which is working the Cotton, that is from the feed roller, round the lickerin to the cylinder and from the cylinder round to the doffer, from the doffer to the doffing comb, that the lickerin itself has more points of wire than there are fibres on the lickerin; that the cylinder has at least four times as many points of wire, and the doffer rather over twice as many; that the flats, viz.: 110 revolving flats, of which 44 are at work, have eight times as many points of wire as there are fibres of cotton on the flats. This table will give the groundwork for a considerable amount of reflection and calculation as to the working of Cotton fibres, and I think it tends to bear out the theory of Carding that is enunciated in my paper. I had occasion to check the correctness of my calculations by the examination of the various Yarns under the microscope, and I found that my calculations were borne out by absolute experiment. I found, however, that the results I arrived at were so different from those hitherto supposed to exist, that on referring to the standard work on the Cotton Fibre, that is *The Structure of the Cotton Fibre*, by Dr F. H. Bowman, I found such a difference between my calculations of the number of fibres in the cross section of the thread and those of Dr. Bowman's that I wrote to this gentleman with a view to having his opinion. He replied to my letter as under :—

" In reply to your favour of the 31st August the tables given in my work on
" the Cotton fibre, page 143, were the result of direct and careful counting.
" I used our own yarn, which was a combed yarn, and made from very fine
" Galini Cotton, and I had no idea there would be such a discrepancy
" between it and the Egyptian which we use for the ordinary carded yarn.
" I have to-day counted the fibres in some of our 62's carded, and found 52,
" 58, 53, 54, which seems to indicate that we are now using a much coarser
" Cotton, than six years ago. I can give no other explanation, for I was
" very careful in the matter and took an average of several countings."

Upon my further examining the matter I found that the yarn spun in the present day is invariably spun with coarser fibre than formerly to such an extent that it would be necessary in order to form an opinion and comparison, to go through the whole of the various counts of yarn and carefully examine them microscopically. There is no difficulty in doing this as the fibres of the yarn are so visible that they can readily be counted. I found for the ordinary 60's carded yarn, out of several examples that I have examined, that the number of fibres in the cross section vary from 35 to 51, showing the great difference of the quality of the fibre employed by different firms. Those of you who have studied Dr. Bowman's book will understand that the strength of yarn does not consist so much in the absolute hard twist of the yarn as from the fact that by twisting the fibres, they interlock with one another from the natural twist existing in the fibre. If the Cotton is plucked unripe it is impossible to twist those fibres which have not ripened sufficient to develop the natural twist, and these fibres, although twisted in for a portion of their length, stand out from the yarn and make what is known as "furry" or "oozy" thread. This also can be very well seen in the microscope, and I have also reason to believe that when Cotton is overcarded, the action of the hard, sharp points of the wire upon the delicate outside waxy cover of the fibres is, to a certain extent, to remove some of the natural twist and the elasticity of the fibre, and I am also of the opinion that this can be carried further to an injurious extent by the subsequent operations in Preparing and Spinning.

The yarn made from properly ripe Cotton with its full quantity of natural twist can be made of a cheaper and shorter fibre, and coarser, and still have the same elasticity and strength as if the Cotton were longer in staple and finer in quality. Thus, for instance, I have tried in the course of my experiments : yarn made from a fibre of 35 to the cross section of 62's, against the yarn having 50 fibres. The yarns were pretty much of the same strength from the fact that the coarser fibre had a good natural twist, and by being more twisted in the Mule, the fibres were more interlocked. At the same time it may be taken as an absolute fact proved by experience and experiment, that a yarn made of the finer fibre will always possess more of those qualities which are desirable for manufacturing than the yarn spun from the coarser fibres. The number of fibres interlocking, and the number of interlocks caused by the natural twist of the fibre are the measure of the elasticity, strength, and roundness of the yarn. This is an additional reason for carrying out the Carding process in such a manner as will least alter the natural appearance and condition of the Cotton fibre taken ripe from the cotton pod.

My experiments also give me reason to reflect with regard to the disposition of the wire in the covering of Engines, that is to say, as to whether they should be Twill, Ribbed, or

Plain, and of course that is a point which also will come more under the scope of a paper on Card Clothing.

Another ample field of investigation which is worth scientifically following is the influence of Carding upon the fact that certain yarns may prove in the single of the proper standard strength and still fail lamentably in the warp, and even more so lamentably when doubled. This question is one that interests everybody engaged in the industry.

Name of Working Part.	Revolutions per Minute.	Diameter in Inches	Circumferential speed in Inches.	Proportionate Speed.	Nos. of Wire Clothing.	No. of Points of Wire on 1 In. x 40 Inches.	Area of Working Parts. sq. Ins.	No. of Points on Working Parts.	No. of Points at Work.	No. of Fibres on Working Parts.	No. of Fibres on 1 in. x 40 Inches.	Waste %
Feed Roller ..	1	2¼	7·068	1	—	—	—	—	—	—	1950066	0·6
Lickerin ..	100	9¼	12252	1733	8	1120	680	34305·6	19040	18819	1107	1·6
Cylinder ..	160	50¼	25504	3608	120	24000	3760	3825600	2256000	49791	5297	2·01
Doffer ..	12	24¾	933	132	130	29000	1760	2254750	1276000	605176	13754	
110 Revolving Flats ..			375	0·53	130	29000	1760	3190000	1276000			3·3
8 Stationary Flats ..					100	21000	400	210000	210000			
8 „ „ ..					110	23000	400	230000	230000			
8 „ „ ..					120	27040	400	270400	270400			
8 „ „ ..					140	28000	400	280000	280000			3·0
Doffing Comb ..	1137	8¼	29472·6	4208	—	—	45	660	660	—	—	—

DOBSON & BARLOW'S
PATENT DOFFING COMB MOTION.

Extract from " The Textile Manufacturer," February 15, 1885.

ONE of those little details about a Carding Engine, apparently very small, but in reality of cardinal importance, upon which the working of the machine depends, is the comb motion for doffing the fleece from the doffer before it is transformed to a sliver at the head of the cam motion. The speed of the engine, and therefore its production, is determined by that of the comb motion; it is possible to run the usual comb motions at extra-ordinary speeds, and therefore to work the engine at an exceedingly good rate for a time. But symptoms of failure will undoubtedly appear in a short time in the comb motion, either on account of the smallness of the wearing surfaces allowing for too rapid wear, or from points in the design of the motion permitting of parts to first wear and then knock together twice for every effective stroke of the comb. Whilst with the usual motions supplied by the ordinary machine makers we have them constructed on these lines showing defects in principle, we have them also designed on lines that involve exact and expensive workmanship to construct them, and some, moreover, that are by no means easy to get together. Mr. DOBSON, of Messrs. DOBSON & BARLOW, Bolton, seeing the drawbacks of the ordinary motions, even for the usual speeds of working, leaving alone the more than usual speeds when adopted, spent some time in designing the arrangement we herewith illustrate, and which as far as we are aware contains a motion that is entirely new. On this ground alone it would be worth description; but as the motion meets effectively the defects usually observed when the ordinary motions are run at high speeds, and as its manufacture is com-paratively easy, there being no hand fitting about it, we think it well worthy of illustration.

Referring to the illustrations, Fig. 1 is an elevation, Fig. 2 a sectional elevation, Fig. 3 another sectional elevation at right angles to Fig. 2, and Fig. 4 a plan with the lid removed. The apparatus is driven by a band on the pulley on the spindle marked a. As seen in Figs. 2 and 3, there is turned solid with this spindle a small eccentric which is enclosed in another eccentric, or rather this larger eccentric is the strap of the smaller one. The shaft c is the comb shaft which it is desired to vibrate; it has fastened to it by the set screw the strap of the larger eccentric. The centres of the spindle a and the comb shaft c are of course stationary, and as the spindle a revolves continuously, the eccentric that revolves with it must vibrate large strap, and therefore the comb shaft. The larger eccentric does not revolve in its strap, but simply works backwards and forwards through a small arc. A very great advantage attached to this motion is, as will be seen, that the work in manufacturing it can all be done with the lathe and planing machine, there being no handfitting required, and therefore interchangeability is very easily obtained. The lubrication of these motions, in view of the great speed at which they run, and the severity of the work they have to perform, is a very important point, and much attention has been given to it in the motion illustrated. The eccentrics work submerged in oil, as shown in Figs. 2 and 3, and with the rapid oscillation of the strap or lever *c* the oil is projected all over the internal cavity of the motion, loss being avoided by the cap which is screwed on the top. The oil then enters the dark grove shown in the plan Fig. 4, and which is on a level with the centre line of the comb shaft, which it thoroughly lubricates, and then falls into the reservoir below. Much the same mode is provided for the oiling of the eccentric spindle *a*; none of the oil can escape along the spindle, it being trapped by the grove shown in the bush. The escape of oil round the bush itself is prevented by a ring of asbestos kept in its place by a screwed gland.

A great merit of this appliance will be at once recognised by our readers. It has no parts projecting from the inside or from the doffer side of the motion, it is therefore much easier to keep clean than those motions in which it is necessary to have projections. Fly and dirt tends to accumulate in the recesses between them, and sometimes enters the engine, which, of course, is not a desirable contingency. At the time of our visit we saw it running extremely well with absolute steadiness—in fact, at 1600 vibrations a minute; and we understand that when one which had been at work for nearly a year at about this speed was taken apart for examination, not the slightest signs of wear could be observed, and it was put together again with the parts in the same condition—a sufficient proof, we think, of its efficiency.

Any of our readers who desire to inspect the motion can, we understand, do so upon application to Messrs. DOBSON & BARLOW, Machinists, Bolton, who, we have no doubt, will be glad to show it to anyone interested.